Journey Backward

Journey Backward
Tom O'Malley

Salmon Poetry

Published in 1998 by
Salmon Publishing Ltd,
Cliffs of Moher, Co. Clare

© Tom O'Malley 1998
The moral right of the author has been asserted.

A catalogue record for this book is available from the British Library.

Salmon Publishing gratefully acknowledges the
financial assistance of the Arts Council.

ISBN 1 897648 14 6 Softcover

All rights reserved. No part of this publication may be reproduced or transmitted in any form or by any means, electronic or mechanical, including photography, recording, or any information storage or retrieval system, without permission in writing from the publisher. The book is sold subject to the condition that it shall not, by way of trade or otherwise, be lent, resold or otherwise circulated without the publisher's prior consent in any form of binding or cover other than that in which it is published and without a similar condition, including this condition, being imposed on the subsequent purchaser.

Cover artwork by Austin Carey
Cover design by Brenda Dermody of Estresso
Set by Siobhán Hutson in Goudy
Printed by Betaprint, Clonshaugh, Dublin 17

For Gabriel, Madge and Micheál

Acknowledgements

Acknowledgement is due to the editors of the following, in which some of these poems have also appeared:

Poetry Ireland Review, *New Irish Writing*, *The Mayo Anthology*, *The Irish Times*, *Exhibit A* (RTE), *The Cafe Review* (USA), and *Quarry* (Canada).

Contents

Lough Mask Lichens	1
Bog Sculpture	3
Found Sculpture	4
Rock Music	5
Shranalong River	6
Ceide Fields	7
Algae	8
Time-Share	9
Viking Graveyard	10
Kattegat and Skagerrak	11
The Cleft	12
Wild Potatoes	13
Gash in Tarmac (Mushrooms)	14
New Year's Eve	15
Inspiration	16
Artefact	17
In Search of Lucás	19
Myles Joyce	21
Seasonal Haiku	22
Spring	22
Summer	23
Autumn	25
Winter	26
Roots and Instincts	27
The Pine	28
The Contract	29
Rivals	30

Travelling Shop	31
In the Garden	32
Ageing Space	33
The Dog	34
The Pike Hunt	35
The Rationing	36
The Rabbit Trap	37
The Mallard	38
By Lough Mask	39
Falcon	40
The Dog-Fox	42
Milking	44
Map Lichens (Co Mayo)	45
Past Masters	47
Clearing Blackthorns	49
Stakes	50
Miracles	51
Sinneán	52
Sight and Sound	53
Sticks for the Reek	55
Skellig Huts	57
Fault	58
Tuber	59
Beech Mast	60
Tap-Root	61
Kavanagh Anniversary '84	62
Ships of Passage	63
Spring Cleaning	64

Premature	65
Science/Magic Haiku Sequence	66
Writing Haiku	67
Garden Fire	68
Liberation	69
Journey Backward	70
Potato	73
Summer Thunder	74
Predator	76
Obsessed with Lichens	78

Lough Mask Lichens
for Patrick Deeley

I've climbed up here, above Lough Mask, to view two tarns
and find a cut-away bog in a mountain hollow.
Lying about, is a galaxy of small round boulders
where lichens rush to put their foot down – firmly
marking out their new won territories on maps, maps
and more maps. Each individual stone is a globe,
a whole new world to be conquered, held, apportioned out,
divided and sub-divided; their settlements
sharply indentured in sepia ink
and brightly coloured with the lichens themselves:

each stone an atlas page, as they chart their known universe.

One map is a world that seems long established –
a monochrome-chart of duns and browns; its indentured
mesh a jigsaw of states; of principalities, dukedoms; even
great empires – the whole interspersed
with bright green inland seas and pale grey lakes.

This other is a glorious chart of dramatic colours –
with vast turquoise oceans; a cloudy land-mass of continents
and sub-continents in vivid orange, rust or grey;
and a scatter of islands in sunbursts of yellow.
Its one immaculate dazzle of white
this creeping floe from its polar icecap.

One small dull map, pale-grey, is flat as its page: you have
to look very closely to see its subtle intermesh
of Aran fields, rectangular, irregular, crowded.
– A ghost survey.

And there is a world just discovered by lichen adventurers –
their new settlements of rust, edging the grey vastness
of unexplored continents; with here and there
tiny patches of black:
the uncharted homelands of its scattered tribes – perhaps.

Bog Sculpture

Bog oak – its shape,
its aura of antiquity
impress the sculptor's eye.

He follows its image-lead.

Hamlet, who saw camels
in cloud, or a weasel
or whale; what would he see,
I wonder, in these
ghastly-white
wood-shapes
the sculptor carves,
smooth-polishes brown,
glosses,
preserves?

Eerily irregular,
his 'bog speak'
fascinates my eye;

touches the very marrow.

Found Sculpture

Only when the Mask sinks low in summer
can you pioneer through shrubs,
round jagged edges of limestone
leaping precariously from rock
to water-hewn rock
to a hidden place, where a stream
finds exit through woods
and stones are sculpted strange shapes
by lake water, stream water, time:
shapes hollowed and holed;
some whitened to Carrara marble,
their spiney surfaces patterned weirdly,
the stream-stroke smoothed,
the current moulded – shapes
that ultimately mean nothing
but themselves,
the exquisitely irregular and fascinating.

Rock Music

Here, blue-grey limestone is sharply cut
into huge cube shapes by Lough Mask water;
their pocked surfaces – spiney egg-trays.

When summer has shrunk the lake to shallows
you trek this way around Ballykine wood,
these water-hewn steps your Giant's Causeway.

Here, most rocks respond to your tapping stick,
not with rock's usual flat stolidity,
but with a faint or a striking resonance.

One, sliced thin from a massive sliced pan,
its end still joined to its loaf of rock,
held the deep toned resonance of solid iron:

from end to end you tapped an octave; and felt
you might have played a tune in it, like
a stage-performer skilled with water bottles.

But most striking – the rough-cut basket of stone
too heavy to lift by its stone handle
which rang with the clarity of bell metal.

Though most responded to your tapping stick,
this, like a tuning fork, held perfect pitch –
by its frozen note you'll judge all rock music.

Shranalong River

You too would have enjoyed this place, Henry Moore:
the stream-bed staired upward with time-hewn locks
and waterfalls, step by step from lake edge to mountain.

We have trekked here in August heat to chill our flesh
and from its green-banked, sheep-grazed heath are aware
that its sculpted depths are cavernous;
its two-way mirror of reflected sky, hiding both the
profundity of its depths and a trout voyeur
that views our world clearly from its pool of light.

In togs and goggles, I wade in and breast-stroke out
drinking, as I go,
cool mountain water – living off the land as it were.

Underwater it's as if a light's switched on – the trout scares
(at the strange white-goggled-monster, I must appear.)

Alone, I savour my fish-tank room where non-stop water
rushes over rockfalls down from Scoltach to my shoulders;
and with its boulder-roll, its pestle-on-mortar effect
scoops out caverned rock.
                        A strange world this, of
female forms – of torsos, firm boobs, haunches, hollows,
thighs – everywhere you look
reclining figures are bathing in shallows,
or at least, some parts of their anatomy.
                        One I photographed:
her hollowed-belly held an infant rock inside, its oval-head
popped out. Her trunk, shoulders, breasts, thighs:

a Henry Moore Madonna, reclining at the side of a rockpool,
near Mary Anne's bridge, on the Shranalong river,
and her fully formed infant getting ready to be born.

Ceide Fields

Surface stones are weathered, even healthy looking
compared with these, prehistoric walls, they exhume
at Belderrig – Neolithic skeletons of expired fields,
now no longer green except to imagination – their walls
bound once with a mesh of ivy-weave; and painted rust,
black, white, grey by daubing lichens' crude artistry;
a sturdy windbreak against Atlantic gales; combed
with briar entanglements and with blackthorn hedgerows.

Today, my eye is shocked by their ghostly pallor,
their dazzling bone-glow among peat workings –
white angels that are too pure for the eye's comfort,
a tabula rasa bleached by the pickling
of five millenia in humic acid – and craving once more
fresh inks of weathering, a green nuance of algae,
the enamelling lichens' multicoloured glaze.

And yet, I must celebrate their geometric patterns
which stamped sharp order on a Mayo wilderness –
their lines, angles, rectangles, squares
shaping uncultured minds as they cultivated space.

Algae

Observing the green stones
of the roofless calf shed
and remembering your son's knees
and togs stained grass-green from play
you thought it was the seeping dyes
of the overhanging sycamore leaves
must have run their pigments onto them
the cut stones were so evenly painted.

Not so: 'algae' you were told –
algae, blown invisibly by the aerosol
of the moist breeze painted
their green graffiti
on these old stone walls.
And was that algae too you recalled
back then on a summer Sunday
polluting a Cavan lake
where trout drowned in a pea-soup fog?

Time-Share

Here, jagged grey limestone rock
is lashed by wintry waters
of Tom Keane's turlough –

a field of waves
he time-shares with
this Lough Mask wilderness.

For over half each year,
a wildlife habitat,
fishermen cast bait there;

but come mid May
swans and wild-duck vacate
their wintry tenancy

as brown-burnt mossy walls
and grass re-appear
above shrunken waters.

The rest of the summer through
Tom's cattle graze
his fluctuant field.

Viking Graveyard
at Aalborg, Denmark
for Mary and Flemming Urth

Antiquity intact,
this Viking graveyard was preserved
by wind-blown sand dunes

until a woman's probing stick
alerted archaeologists.
Now, all lies open, bare,

'interpreted' – pagan graves
with high stone prows, high sterns;
low ribs of stone.

Infatuated with their oared craft,
their lithe sea-steeds of discovery,
of piracy and commerce,

they chose cremation within
these ritual ship-shapes.
And what better craft

to sail their adventurous spirits
to uncharted Valhalla
than these mythic stone ships

evocative of wood's resonance
to the wave's turbulence –
the creaking of oars.

Kattegat and Skagerrak
North Denmark

Through winds ghosted with blown sands,
eyes shielded; our bare legs, bare arms
sand-blasted, we tourist-trek up the long beach
to watch chill waves charge east
charge west, where the North Sea meets Baltic,
and tides reassert their precise boundaries.

Here in Skagan light that painters celebrate,
you catch on vivid photograph
that single white blossom of billow
reared by the clashing of two matched forces.

I think of frontiers defined on maps –
the scribble of rivers, the Sahara sands, perhaps;
coastlines, mountains and that arbitrary
disputed frontier between South and North
which even cuts through farms – and am struck
by this 'cold war' equilibrium achieved by tides
as two mighty forces, fluid but exact,
affirm a lunar contract endorsed on water.

Here, East is East definitively and West, West
as Kattegat co-exists with Skagerrak.

The Cleft

Defying the August droughts
this rock cleft was our unfailing spring,
a village dug

when quarried wells dried up
and our saucers scooped out more silt
than water. Then, tin cans slung

from Raleigh handlebars,
we queued at this rock cleft
so narrow, only bent pea-tins fitted.

Yet, no matter how much water
we measured into vessels,
its high winter-levels kept.

Nor did we think to ask
the why of this or tamper with crow-bar
or sledge – but accepted

how the gift was given –
doled unstintingly but in small measures.
And although a certain dread

hovered for us among its dank,
dark hawthorn shadows, its brimming cup
was our potent source

of earth's numinous resurgence.

Wild Potatoes

It is these 'wild' potato stalks that delight the
hunter/gatherer in you more than the sown ridge;
as here and there, among your rows of propped peas
the unsown, random, green-feathered stalks
sit on the summer soil like Rhode Island Reds
in the dry dust-dents of their own scratchings.

You have taken a blue bucket, a garden spade
and turned out their secret nests, full of oval
creamy-gold nuggets – the unearned, the undeserved,
evocative of potatoes' wild habitat among the Andes,
the red hen's hankering for laying out in grass.

Gash in Tarmac (Mushrooms)

Shoulder to shoulder
with a joint effort
they head-butt upwards

a shoe-sole of tarmac,
and throw it aside.

From trapdoors of Hades,
raised subterranean heads
appal us with their
netherworld pallor, their

insidious upheaval
right on our doorstep,
before they blacken back

down to their world.

We seal off their exit,
their gash in tarmac, with
vain sweepings of gravel,

stamped tight – unsure now
when they'll strike next ,
or where. They've breached

our higher defences;
unsettled our faith.

New Year's Eve

It is New Year's Eve
nineteen ninety four
dusk thickening
in the Meath fields;
the road I walk
is black with ice,
my face is a mask
of frozen epidermis,
my coat, my scarf snug.
Over the hedge, a herd,
a dozen bullocks
standing to be foddered;
close by, a tractor
with green-hooded cab
its tall fork-lift up
like a praying mantis
against the sky; there is
no driver near; just
a radio or tape
blaring out pop hits
at the centre of a Meath field
towards dusk, New Year's Eve
nineteen ninety four
and cattle listening.

Inspiration

After I opened
my study window,
an in-rushing
breeze
cast back
the hard cover
of my dictionary
over the edge
of my desk.
Before I could
close it
a ghostly thumb
flivelled
its crisp pages
to find
the centre;
after which
the heavy book
somersaulted
onto my carpet –
suggesting
some principle
or proverb, to do
perhaps, with
'first steps'
'the thin end'
'majority decisions';
fasces,
falling apples,
Newton or
Archimedes –

but I'll leave it.

Artefact
for Ruth

While trowelling out
old lily roots
Jim spotted it –
the clay-filled round
a golden artefact;
'Twenty two carat,'
his mother said
recalling it; and
remembering too
Granny's loss and their
inch by inch search
through lawn grass
back then; and Granny's
fuss, obsessive
as a ghost, haunting
some place of grief,
her bleary eyes
forever on look-out
around flower-beds,
under laurel leaves
for that union band –

and dreading some omen.

In a matchbox
among dresser cups
it remained two weeks:
a conversation-piece.

Evoking ghosts
it re-peopled the house
with previous owners
(faded in photographs)
until one morning:
panic – gone –
no one knows where;
unless, yes, her son
now eighty eight
and absent minded
finding no match
cast it in the fire.

The ashes is searched;
the ash-pit sifted
and sifted through,
but there is no sign,
no glint of gold: all
mysteriously vanished;

the ghosts too.

In Search of Lucás
(great-grandfather)

With crow-bar and sledge
and four muscular sons
he wrested
a limestone farm
from the Lough Mask wilderness.

So much for hearsay.

For the rest
an archaeologist of sorts
I visit the site –
my search for artefacts,
a search for roots.

A primary source – his house;
still sturdy:
thatched once, but now
sheeted with galvanise
to winter calves.
'A cut above the average,' I'd say
with its cut-stone chimney,
chimney breast
and fireplace.

His farm itself –
My eyes follow its three
peninsulas of wrested grass:
three flat green webs
between long fingers of rock.

Taller than warranted, I feel,
are his dry-limestone walls,
absorbing, perhaps,
some excess of his quarried outcrop.
His scatter of carraigáns
on waste – small cairns now
to his buried energy.

At last, behind hazel scrub, I find it –
the 'bull ring'
my father talked of –
a drystone 'amphitheatre' Lucás built
and where cows were served.

Who kept a bull was a man apart.

I climb its limestone wall
as circular and thick
as a Bronze Age fort – and wonder
what future archaeologists
will make of it.

He broke the land's back
and made his mark. They say
three of his sons left
and were never heard of.

On his drumlin's height
a single molar of rock stands
gum-bedded yet
beyond stir of his crow-bar.
I firm it in memory now
to be his menhir.

Myles Joyce
(Hanged 1882, for the Maumtrasna murders, but believed innocent)

Fingered by crown approvers; sold
to imperial justice for immunity
and gold, he walks, hands tied
from his cell in Galway –
a confessed murderer on either side.

It is 1882 and Myles Joyce
grieves from the scaffold
for his orphaned children.
From the gallows' height
he protests his innocence
to the watching journalists,
utterly beyond earshot
of his alien gaelic.

The jury at Green Street
have found him guilty; so what
fault theirs if the evidence is false.
'I go to meet Christ's face,'
he bellows in gaelic, 'another
betrayed, though innocent; he
at least, understands my plight.'

The rope snakes round him
as he still gesticulates:
a clatter of bolts, and all three
are shot through – two, their
necks broken, die instantly;
the third writhes, strangling
slowly in the agony of the crucified;

and that man is Myles Joyce.

Seasonal Haiku

Spring Haiku

Another rite of spring –
as clocks move forward one hour
we take the fast lane.

>I clear a patch
>for seeds and seedlings – the weeds
>have their own agenda.

Tall April birch trees –
sterling silver by moonlight:
white barks hall-marked.

>Moon-powered, hydraulic –
>this 'spring' tide jacks up moored ships,
>yachts, fishing trawlers.

Beamed to chancel wall –
stained glass negatives of saints:
medieval slides.

>Communion faces –
>pink, green, orange, red and blue –
>sun through rose window.

A bright amber glow
on the rim of Ben Chorcaigh;
– then the moon rises.

Summer Haiku

Close up – these seagulls
that follow our boat; no need
for binoculars.

    After her swim, she
    sits by the pool – skin varnished
    by water-glaze.

His water-marked arm:
'Authentic health,' declare two
vaccination stamps.

    Cicadas clicking
    throughout the hot Spanish night
    – can't find even one.

Venus-vowelled – these
phoned business secretaries;
with perfumed voices.

    Lovers at airport
    part reluctantly – velcro
    slowly separates.

On the weather chart,
a criminal's finger print –
Hurricane Charlie?

His farmhouse and sheds
a crannóg (these floods) – he rows
pike meadows, herds swans.

>   Troubled, he wanders
>   about the Lough Mask landscape
>   – a sick dog bites grass.

My wilderness walk:
two screeching seagulls swoop-
dive their predator.

>   After rain: on my
>   cabbage leaves' dry stream beds
>   – drops of quicksilver.

Down steep Ben Chorcaigh
a sheep-glacier's slow progress
– shearing tomorrow.

>   Red evening sunbeams –
>   the white breast of our kitten
>   is pink tinctured.

Scared – our grey cat
defines a gothic arch
with her humped back.

>   Dead roadside fox – gone
>   his mystery, ghostly sightings;
>   we turn away.

Autumn Haiku

Autumn mist – its grey
string-beads betray the spider's
crafty hammocks.

> Indian summer –
> rusted leaves float on the warm
> river we swim in.

October's breath –
a powder blue mist on sloes
takes my finger print.

> Stiff from the iron
> your cool white bed linen
> – faint scent of metal.

Carpet fawns and browns
blent with crisp birch leaves, blown in
– my autumn hallway.

> Beyond Gropius:
> their design and function one
> – turf stack and hay stack.

Their gradual heights –
propped pea rows graph my garden's
micro climates.

Winter Haiku

A sodden moss nest
in the fork of a sceach
– cradles rusty leaves.

> November: full moon –
> sketched charcoal ash trees
> on the frosty road.

The air warm again –
children's snow sculptures deflate
in green/white gardens.

> The windy creaking
> of this ivy hooded sceach –
> winter's key-note.

A cold season's breath
from my freezer's open door
– winter's kept on ice.

> Amundsen and Scott –
> algae and lichen compete
> for the South Pole.

Amplified by frost –
from Ballykine wood at dusk
snarls of a chainsaw.

Roots and Instincts

Grey-frigid, he stands out on a hard landscape
of streaked limestone, beside a glacial lake,
as stark as in some drawing by Edvard Munch.
He seems to lack all fruitful contact with rich soil,
tribal warmth or touch of a gentle god; and yet
he survives, absorbing sustenance like this ash
that persists, though stunted, in mysterious clefts
where no life is normally expected. I wonder at
the ingenuity of these roots, their prospecting instinct
that can suck up food from some secret source. What
brute will lives deep in both their natures
that can give them energy to live though warped – the ash
in its dwarfed ashness, he in his stark humanity.
And yet, both endure and somehow proclaim life
where white rock is chill even at high summer.

The Pine

Testing for some ancient god of trees
I circle two fully grown arms around
the crusted girth of a tall pine
that stands erect by the cow-house gable.
I look upwards along its scaled bark
to where blue-grey tufts lather white
foam onto the sky's face and sense only
you, father, your sinewed, pliant strength,
all masculine uprightness.
Years shed, as boyhood's fingers grip
closer still about your fibrous waist
feeling flesh-firmness, the strong-grained
rhythm of ribs, muscle-knots of grace.
Remote above my head, I sense your gaze
far out over the lake, yet cling for solace
knowing hard bark belies the sap-thrust
up long bole and branch to glossed tufts.

The Contract

Some age-old contract, often hinted at,
appears in sleep out of antique mists at night:
a blood-sealed, worn out, covenant
on timeless parchment, yellowed, almost black.

What it signifies is not revealed. I glimpse
mysterious hieroglyphics, thin, italicised,
full of magic hints and formulae, stronger
than druids ever knew – divine imprints.

Flourished before my eyes, I reach out – in vain
as two authoritative white hands tear it
ruthlessly across; his eyes full of warnings;
his threatening finger saying I'm to blame.

Then, I rack my brains to find just what
exactly it is that I have lost. It's not my house:
the deeds are safe. It's not my wife, or job;
but yet I feel an age-old broken contract.

Rivals

The twenties were arrogant times
when the priest valued his status.
One, on hearing of your grandfather's
cooper's skills from awed villagers,
called in one day at his shop
to watch the cooper at work in the yard
hooping the timber slats into place
and making the whole watertight.
'Not much to it really, Mick,' he patronised
'except of course for the *lattin*.'

Quick as a flash the craftsman's pride
hit back: 'And except for the Latin,
father, what's there to saying mass?'

Travelling Shop

That winter's night in the light of the shop
window, we helped, as usual, unload the van.
You had come back, tired, from your mountain run
and were busy counting your takings into the till.

We lifted out the unsold goods: the sugar
in brown paperbags, the cardboard boxes of tea,
cornflakes, custards, jellies, bread and jam
and then we tried our strength on the heavyweights.

We were never really short of sweets and biscuits:
your shelves were our orchard and forbidden fruit
found many ways to our jacket pockets; though
not without guilt – I wonder if you really knew.

That evening, I'll never know why, when our work
was done, you gave us two red apples each:
I locked mine in a biscuit tin for a week –
trying to preserve the gesture, not the fruit.

In the Garden

I watch my father shovel up the loose clay
of the vegetable plot. He levers it deftly
casting the cold mould onto the spring ridge.
Suddenly appears the green shell of a tortoise,
all dirtied now, mine once thirty years back.

I'm quietly sitting, aged five, under the red
beam of evening sunlight, by our back west-window,
totally absorbed in its head-nodding mystery.

His shovel clanks an old clay pipe, earth dyed.
I lift it and note where the brittle stem snapped.

My grandfather sits by an open kitchen fire
telling stories of wakes with irreverent mirth,
the corpse of a neighbour propped on a bed.

Hair-cracked bits of Victorian delft lie scattered
among the ridge pebbles: I note their willow pattern.

God knows for how long this tiny earth patch
has sustained our family going back and back. I see
our relics still retained by clay: yes, the earth
has given, then takes – I'm already half there.

Ageing Space

Thinking of retirement, I consider joining you
'hale and hearty' and eighty two, in that twilight zone
between the workaday world and the unknown country.
You lead me again – age following the more aged,
as you led me once – youth following matured youth
when we humped jute sacks of two hundred weight, you
at one end, I the other, onto a horsecart; or
working in tandem, both of us equally fit,
queued up at your lorry to take them on our backs.

Our lives pattern strangely: continue to intersect.

And then you retired, well semi-retired, entered age;
began the gradual process of decline – not of mind,
    certainly:
still you devour newspapers; and talk of world affairs
as if an expert. Though today less steady on your feet
you cycle miles to count your cattle, argue, fuss; keep
your hand in, casting a dash of wisdom on our 'youth'.

And now I stand bemused on the threshold of that world
savouring life's ironies – father and son
both pensioned off, both ageing: the grey and greyer,
senior and more senior; flesh weakening at joints.
How will we relate; which has more wisdom now both
    have aged?
Is the child father of the man or still child of the father?
Or is there space enough for both in that zone also?

The Dog

After that officious envelope with wrong receipts,
we wasted the cool gracious afternoon, in hot
frustrated argument, over some computer's far-off,
arrogant disrespect for mere blood and flesh.

Towards dusk, you got your coat and gloves, I mine
and walked, still bothered, down the narrow roadway;
frost half-thawed glistening in the hedge's shadow,
the air towards freezing point, cooling us both.

You remember, passing that farmhouse, a grey dog,
huge, with short hair, blocking our path; his grin
a mask of malice that sent a chill up my spine
as fierce prelude to some primitive encounter.

He was all wolf then, guarding his gate, canines
bared, his black salivating lips drawn back;
hair raised, snarling fiercely, snapping your heels.
I felt then, but one step from caveman, one step

from that rock that would split his forehead in
if he failed to reach my jugular first. Yet,
we both somehow managed to conform to habit –
It seems the forty centuries we've both been tamed

must count for something. We observed grudging decorum:
he made respectful gestures, let us pass; I let
the fierce ice thaw, half wishing for that ancient contest
with flesh, blood, hair, teeth, rock in savage directness.

The Pike Hunt

After weeks of frost, Lough Carra lay
glinting like steel in February sunlight. Three
inches of plate glass had polished its surface.
Big Mick skidded his van down to the lake edge
and belted the ice with a six pound sledge
that only powdered its point of impact.
No crack appeared even when his men hurled out
huge rocks that soon skated to a halt.
Local boys, off school for Saturday,
began to cycle across; so just for the crack
Mike drove his van out and took a photograph.
'Right,' he said, 'get the buckets men and gaffs.'
And armed with hay-forks, clubs and hatchets
they fanned out.
                    Soon, 'Over here,' one shouted.
We saw pike-shape magnified against the ice
as Mick lifted his club and smashed hard
above the resting forehead. Panicked, the green fish
shot off as the slithering gang, yelping, followed.
'He's here'; but now exhausted he hugs the marl.
'Quick men, dig him out.' Peter, skillful
as a hunting Eskimo, chips a round hole
and Mick's fork prongs him to the bottom.

A silver gaff probes for gills – and slowly
out he's hauled, green-slimed, gob-mouthed,
to lash for life about the glittering surface.

The Rationing

The war in Europe left us undisturbed,
except that food was scarce; so five men gathered,
one summer's evening full of thunder clouds,
to solve the problem. I was in the house

when a pig's wild screech pierced the village air:
my dog slunk quietly to his corner, hair
on end. Abroad, the sky looked ominous
but dry, as flocks of crows took off in terror.

When I arrived, I found the white pig tied
and stretched on a door across two barrels.
About, were buckets full of water, two knives,
and a basin to hold the blood of sacrifice.

Four men held down his white length, while one,
who had often played with me and swung me round,
took the sharpest knife and cut a thin slit,
clean and white on the pig's white throat –

then plunged it screaming in, as red poured out
and down to the battered basin by his side.
The wildly pumping heart did all the rest,
as soon the screeching pig sagged flat and died.

It was my first taste of death; so I looked on
half awed, half terrified – my five years
shattered by the actions of these men I'd loved
but could never trust completely afterwards.

Later, I read at school about the war,
the rationing, the dead of Poland, Russia;
but most of all of Dachau, Belsen, Auschwitz –
and somehow, I seemed to understand it all.

The Rabbit Trap
for Fergal Giles

When his foot dropped on this metal plate
last night, the iron teeth gripped.
It seems that whoever invented it sought
only to abstract the bare essentials of
some predator's mouth – with pliant springs
replacing muscles and iron jaws
lined with teeth. He even placed a
metal tongue at the centre, as if
to taste how warm the blood is. Yet,
he left no body, no throbbing lust for flesh:
just an iron grip, a metal reflex.

The Mallard

On the kitchen table, under the harsh light,
the wild-duck lies, a green sheen on its stiff neck;
the rust-webbed feet are crinkled, tense in death.
You said how you raised it from the shore at dusk
and lifted your metallic gun-barrel after it:
a harsh explosion belled your ear as the stock
kicked and your spray of pellets outstripped its panic.
Now, the sharp eye is tight-lidded, that lemon beak
is badly chipped; but yet as if it still wished
to hide beneath soft down that gross entrance which
your pellets made, the stiff wing lies folded.

We are hunters, both. You with your rods, gun, traps
and bait express your nature, lore and prowess
but capture death. I must try in words to catch
that something most elusive your pellets missed
as wild and shy, the squawking mallard rose
abruptly up from lawn grass – to a grand, majestic
flapping into twilight, its graceful neck outstretched,
its webbed feet flush with its smooth undercarriage.

By Lough Mask

Concealed by brown erratics,
four brown hares cock their ears
at my footstep on white limestone
left bare since the last ice-age.

'Halloed', their hind-legs pump
over the white landscape,
past briars and hazel clumps;
then merge again with boulders.

A wild-duck wings vigorously in
low over tree tops, to land
beside me on the lake; sees me
and veers abruptly left

with rapid wing-flaps. I feel
let down, an intruder. Surprised
by the swish of my boots in long grass
a fox ignites rust-red and skips

quietly off to his thicket.
Of what does he suspect me?
Surely, I admire him – and yet
perhaps he's wise not to trust.

Falcon

Observe the falcon, his sickle beak
up-ripping the gull's white plumage
unstitching smooth seams.

Admire his high perch among
fawn rocks of his texture,
the dark pool of his pupil

whose telescopic lens scans
earth, sea and air
just to practise his terror.

The salt tang of flesh,
the raw blood of birds,
with talons outstretched,
he grips, with a shriek.

They well-up his energy,
relustre his plumes,
find a nobler existence
in his muscle and sinew.

A solitary always, he needs no friend;
watch gull-flocks scatter in
white clouds before him.

A disciple of Nietzsche, an Aryan
blue-blood, he vents contempt
on mere pigeons or crows.

His dive is a blitzkrieg, a quick
bolt from the blue
on the back of a ditch-rat.

Small-kin to the eagle, tough
neighbourhood bully
he admits no Godhead, but

plucks fresh wool off the back
or the soft warm breast
of rabbit or leveret.

The Dog-Fox
(*Toby*)
for Kevin and Mary

I.
Began as a blind cub
John dug from its den
and cradled home;

A Jack Russell bitch
that had lost two pups
reluctantly gave suck.

The fox grew up with
two farmyard dogs –
ate with them,

slept with them; once only
did he fight them off
over dinner scraps.

Like a dog, he fussed
and barked – he licked
the faces of children

who led him on walks:
they loved his antics,
forgave his stink.

Though he often ganged
with the farmyard dogs
to chase their grey cat

consider this tableau –
black dog, red fox, cat
snuggled together

in John's turf-shed;
like lion and lamb
transcending instinct.

II
Possessed, one day
he started to den
in John's back garden.

Now, only at night
was he heard to frolic
with Spot or Tim

though Teresa's voice
could still conjure him
for bread or meat –

'till the urge to mate:
a moon-tug on ever
increasing tides –

he spilled one night
over garden walls
into fields – uncharted.

Milking

That morning a winter's ice was on the water trough.
You punched a hole in its glaze and held up
a shining piece to the light as the red cow poked
her tentative nose through the hole you'd made
and gulped down huge chilled gulps. You warmed
your hands on her firm hide; then, pushed her off
to let the others drink. It was like pushing a
hillock – her stubborn flesh as weighted as earth
though gentle and warm. While milking, too,
your forehead rested against her firm flank
as the bubbling whiteness rose in foaming buckets.
Soon, your four fingers tingled, sucked by her calf,
as you directed his teasing gums to the white fluid:
all satiating some instinct, vestigial, sensuous.
Then buckets clanked with a more vibrant music,
your boots clattered harder on the frosty road; and
despite that frost, your overcoat felt warmer
than it does now, removed, literate, aware of a void.

Map Lichens (Co Mayo)
(Rhizocarpo Geographicum)

Between two dark tarns –
a scatter of brown erratics,
each with ethnic murals –

Hair-cracked frescoes
of high mountain lichens,
they demand inspection

where an ink-black thallus
graphically indentures
quaint jig-saw colonies –

make-believe worlds
where each principality, each state
is definitively

pigmented – white, black,
ochre, orange,
duckegg blue ....

One – a Mappa Mundi
of two vast continents,
the faded rust and dotted grey

their tectonic plates
about to collide or drift
on seas of thallus.

This floating white – pristine
snows of Antarctica;
but more exquisite –

in sepia outline, in subtly
shaded fawns and browns,
the surveyed fields

of a Mayo townland –
left hauntingly incomplete
with its marginal wilderness.

Past Masters
for Tom Duddy

You ploughed
a straight furrow
in their small fields.

No spade sliced lea ground
for ridge or drill
without that

plumb-line accuracy
of a taut twine, stretched
peg to peg. Their haycocks

were combed neat,
and butts trimmed
with a barber shop's

precision; then, tightly
roped and scarfed
with canvas sacks.

There was a craftmanship
and pride
in their harvesting; 'Woe

betide' that boy
who could not make
a tight-waisted sheaf

or a stook that stood
regimentally erect
as if on parade. Indeed,

their stubbled fields
were aesthetic sights
at harvest time, for

conservative in taste,
they demanded symmetry –
these Old Masters,

about whose house or haggard
golden stacks were
thatched as if to be

inhabited; their sheep-cocks
proudly masted
with tall poles of larch

to ride out winter;
their long turf-stacks
by garden wall or gable

a delight of masonry,
brown brick by brown brick
handled lovingly;

and then straw-roofed
to cast the excess
of winter's water off.

Clearing Blackthorns

The blackthorn is a stubborn bush, with long toe-roots
spread out witch-like. You pull at them and tug
'till your back breaks. Their great claws seem to grip
earth-flesh as if they clasped the barely underlying rocks.

Like hawks, ravenous, they swallow up your shallow
loam and show a hawk-like arrogance – an ancient
hostility of spikes that tears the flesh of all comers.
Shrewdly, they associate themselves with ring forts

and primitive superstitions; they thrive on soft flesh
or good earth. While of a winter's night, sinister,
druidic, with sharp nails that fright, they send
chill terror up the spines of lonely travellers.

Their gnarled shapes, all knotted, one associates
with pike or shark – chill-blooded monsters. Though
in May glorious, with their tiny, delicate, green leaves,
a spring luxuriance of white, don't be deceived

by Circe dressed for mating. Their fruit is bitter
always – nothing sweet is ever offered but gall,
thorns, spikes. Indeed they are all here:
the totally stubborn, always self-regarding primitive.

Stakes

Standing on an empty tar-barrel
at his yard gate, Tomás bush-sawed off
the lower branches of his
overhanging pussy willow.
He chopped their thicker limbs
into five foot lengths
and slashed them clean with a bill-hook.

One by one he sledged his pile deep
in the sandy ditch along
his mountain road; and stapled up
new rolls of gleaming sheep mesh
– against his black faced ewes.

His green-barked stakes, he said
required no creosote:
their preservative – the sap
that shoots out root and leafage.

Miracles

We collected the hen eggs
Holy Thursday
on grand-dad's advice
and preserved those
laid Good Friday
in a chocolate box
sunk in dried oats –
they would keep
from Good Friday
to Good Friday, he said;
and to test their
freshness he'd circle
each with his fingers
and look through them
at the sun
as through a telescope.
'They're still perfect,'
he'd assure us; and we
believed him; still,
scared perhaps or as
an expression of doubt
we'd never eat them.
'You have to rise early
to see the sun dance
on Easter morning,' he'd
tell us. But we, no matter
how hard we tried
were never able to rise
quite early enough.

Sinneán

The steam of the breeze
has its eddies, the little
whirlpools of current
that a river has.

Sometimes, in a hayfield
white wisps would rise up
and whirl about as if
a mad dog chased its own tail.

Gaoth na Sióga
is what our superstitious
grandfathers called it; but
lacking, perhaps, their

poetic, their animating gifts
we may eventually let
all such rarities slip
with cuckoo and corncrake.

Sight and Sound

As children
we were told to time
the interval

between the forked flicker
that crossed
the spark-gap

between sky and earth
and its re-echoing
racket

as it tore
through our atmosphere;
each second

erroneously believed
to represent
one mile.

But sometimes, sight
and sound
were synchronised

as overhead, a volley
rattled
in your roof tiles

making your home
a sounding-board
of house walls

that stirred up dormant
feelings – atavistic,
perhaps numinous.

Yet, the disparity
between both senses
did not strike

as vividly then
as when you watched
Pat Shaughnessy

splitting blocks
at the upper end
of your village, his

swung hatchet
baulked in wood;
and that mini-second

hiatus, before its
muted thud
reached your ears –

Like a badly dubbed video
each interval
of silence magnified

by expectation.

Sticks for the Reek

On a dark night – sticks for the reek; sticks
for the reek; as John and I prop Raleigh bikes
against a pub in Murrisk. By shunting carlights

we thong tight our boots, lean on peeled ash
and head for the wilderness. Eager for the
summit, we shirk the station round the statue

and tangent upwards, flashlamps, lime-lighting
bare feet, snail-sensitive, picking each tentative
footstep, as our rough hobnails clatter the wet

quartz of Mayo's Golgotha. Gradually, coats soak
as our upward trudge tunnels through mist;
wetness dribbles under collars – our backs

goose-pimple to each flagellating gust. Like Lear
and his fool 'poor forked animals' we re-discover
'the art of our necessities' is strange indeed

as we probe for coins in mist-drenched pockets
and palates savour the tepid tea, smoke-brewed
by huxters under jute-sack awnings. Without

wall of bush for shelter, flesh cowers, craving
the acrid heat of a few itinerant peat-sods
that smoulder feebly in a tent of canvas.

Denied, we mutter aves into the breeze, as we
hobble round the summit with our rosary beads ...

Towards dawn we begin our slow descent from clouds
against a stream of upward-struggling pilgrims –
feet gored, ankles muddied, shoes in tatters;

'till pain absorbed by the scapegoat mountain,
squall asperged,we watch from foothills, green
enchanted islands gracing Clew Bay – and sunlight rising.

Skellig Huts

Tonsure topped –
these wind-swept,
ghostly shells
of Skellig Mhichil:
a rock clutch
of some archaic seabird,
its nestlings, long since
hatched, fledged and
flown off out of history –
leaving but cracked shells
of that exotic species,
transcendentalist;
now as legendary
in tourist lore, as
Phoenix or dodo – men who
so flagellated flesh
on this bleak outpost,
they might, conceivably, have
insinuated themselves
through the needle's eye,
back to nature's
melting pot ..... there
to shape themselves anew
in their maker's image.

Fault

Perhaps, at some lucky moment,
when the fault of middle years
has exposed the cliff-face strata
of self, you'll search the base-scree
'till you chance upon some fossil
dropped once in childhood's sediment.
Chip it off the base-rock, polish up
its blue-grey whorl and then wait
'till memory's magic oozes back
soft suction pads – its twin, pale
antlers scanning perplexed as it
repursues its long arrested progress.

Tuber

All that springtime energy the dahlia
shot up stiff-stem and green leaf
to pink summer with radiant disks
shrank back at winter's first nip –
slimed utterly down to its clay bed:
the destruction of its pride – absolute.

Under the ground a tuber hibernates;
its wrinkled purse leathery with age,
brown as the clay itself is brown –
stained with earth's ancestral pigments:
its life shrunk back to barest elements –
a mere scrotum of hope whose one
shut eye envisions infinite futurity.

Beech Mast

The husks are all
empty; their crisp
shells crackle
under my foot. Through
wide-yawned casing,
their kernels
have all escaped:
each shell a tomb
the God has left.
Look – an angel
of light in every
nook – no flesh and
no death.
      Who was it
stole the body?
And who can guard
a tomb like this?

Tap-Root

I hear the tap-root vibrate off rock
with a tip-tap irate urge to seek, search,
penetrate; always nosing and nibbling with
its shrew's snout the tiny grit of food
this sparse earth allows. Under stones,
mole-blind, in the mole's urgent mode,
it tunnels loam in a constant forage. Home
in the dark clay, it copes with stones
strewn in its path – twists, turns, is
ravenous always; its cunning nose probing
down with dark instinctive force, as it
itches out fresh grit from its deepest source.

Kavanagh Anniversary '84
for the Quinn family, Inniskeen

Muffled in his winter overcoat, Daig
plucked tight weeds while I pinched out
stray scutch from your crazy paving; your
memorial coulter is already rust-pocked.

Beneath our knees your bones had mixed
with your beloved stony matrix,
but today your ears seemed clay-deaf
to our brief ritual of poems and praise.

Yet, after the hot soup and sandwiches
rough, Monaghan accents, on stage,
resurrected your gay spirit. We sat
applauding the furthering of your myth:

heard Tarry Flynn's bright hobnails kick
fresh sparks off the Mucker roadway.
Yes, a summer morning will, undoubtedly,
find you shovelling up eels again

and again as often as your words
are made flesh. Your roots spread far
like antlered whins', on native drumlins
each April barbs with saffron.

Ships of Passage

They pass each other by on Kennedy Street;
he calls 'Howya Mary' as they pass.

His greeting, a line that grapples a passing ship,
they both look backward for five paces.

His line tautened, the two ships drift closer:
words, smiles, a joke exchange.

Then, quietly retrieving his grappling iron,
they drift apart again.

Spring Cleaning
for Anne

Often things have to get worse before getting better
as now, when you blur your side; I, mine.

You polish the windolene into the glass;
and I shine and shine until my blur is gone.

You point out some small imperfection, my side;
I point to a small speck on yours.

Again, we each shine away our observed blemishes
until at last one pane stands perfect between us.

Premature

Daughter, with wet-slimed hair and
elongated shape, with legs pink-purple,
a downey face and fuzzy shoulders
and mouth sucking like a weakened trout
plucked from its true element – so,
dramatically, we meet at this
clinic table in the white glare of lights.

Still womb-damp but, thankfully, intact
your forecast, scanned death is receding hourly.

Detached now, umbilical cut, a green
bubble of fluid floats on your stomach.

In awe, I touch your damp, crimped forehead;
feel your skinny legs that stir towards freedom.

Soon, induced milk from your mother's breasts
will drip slowly down the long tube
you'll worm deep to your gut, as daily
you grow closer and closer to us,
straight from that mystical abyss of daughterhood.

– Joyously, you father and mother us.

Science/Magic (Haiku Sequence)

What poets fantasised,
what sorcerers merely faked
– science brings to birth.

> Paris, his smart-shaft
> finding its precise target
> – Homer's prophesy?

Science commences
with its alchemical search
– for gold; for magic.

> Magic and science
> differ in this: – science must
> realise its tricks.

Keep your fake magic
charlatan witch – that my flicked
light-switch banishes.

> 'Open Sesame',
> Marconi says; and Bell; and
> Baird – and lo, it does.

In space – foetal still,
umbilically attached,
a man crawls weightless.

Writing Haiku

How many odes to
one epic? Sonnets to an ode?
What's one haiku worth?

> Pull? draw? tug? drag? pluck?
> a child seeks le mot juste;
> Flaubert masters prose.

'Give up the day-job? ...
Write poetry? ... Survive with
just a fishing rod?'

> Poet? A mug, says
> Eliot – his own stigma masked
> by his pinstriped suit.

I research grey lobes
of old newspapers – nation's
short-term memory.

> Tiny alphabet –
> millions and millions of words;
> many languages.

I tune my own words
by curtly solid objects –
wood's resonance; rock's.

Garden Fire

I've stacked my garden fire
with old magazines, old newspapers.
Though the flames seem overpowered
they climb upwards round charred edges
leafing away each topmost page
which scrolls back inward on itself.

Methodically the orange flames
devour our yesterdays' stale news,
the glossy ads for motor cars,
the low-cut, high-fashion dresses;
models flaring now, as never before.

Yet sometimes leaving undigested
a weird residue of ashen negatives –
columns of tabloid trivia, headlines, ads
which I re-read clearly as at first
in ghostly print still vivid as if unburnt.

In curious disbelief, I prod a page.
It stains my finger tips
with its grey ashes. I watch it crumble
under pressure into jigsaw flakes
which the spring-gusts catch
scattering their disjointed words
among apple trees and young fruit bushes.

Liberation

Watching TV

a sea-horse
and 'sea-mare'
in their
mating ritual.

His white tail
spirals about
a stem
of green sea-grass.

She gracefully
ballet dances
around his
horse shape.

Corrugated belly
to belly
they mate, she
ovulating into his
inseminating pouch.

Life gestated, he
in time gives
spasmodic birth
to innumerable
'sea-foals'.

My mate, watching
the programme
comments: 'Now there
is real progress.'

Journey Backward
for Gabriel Keane

I
A damp July day, the Mayo sky moss-wet,
We pin-point Glenuwough on the map – its remote
Mountain tarn legendary for brown trout.

II
With fly rods rattling on the Mini's blue roof
We grind in second gear up mountain roads
Westwards through the Partry Range. Beside us
Shrill ravines, their deep-down waters sloshing
Peat brown boulders. Behind, the outstretched Mask
In pewter grey, its islands diminished, telescoped
Closer. Then, downhill all the way as we enter the
    Errif moor,
Bog-fastness of Mayo's pristine interior. Cottages
Approach us, as slowly recede: sheep sprout
In white fungi colonies. Ahead, Crough Patrick nods
Northwards towards Nephin; while to the south
Killary's triangle of light gleams bright
Between dark Ben Gorm and Devilsmother. Out
From inhospitable farm-gates black sheepdogs
Issue, teeth intent on tyres, 'till 'Up there,'
A woman points, 'Lough Glenuwough; about eight
Hundred feet up – good for wild mountain trout!'

III
Hampered by our tackle, green wellingtons, coats
We clamber over the slimy rock-juts, as sweat
And Atlantic wind conspire to irritate.

IV
Summitted, we view the hag-valley of green marsh
Ramparted by mountains – the tarn, a cauldron
In the caverned lap of the great cliff-matriarch.

V
We trudge up the glacial apron, past lilies
Sinister as serpents in abandoned workings,
The sphagnum mosses clumped like rotted tree-stumps.
With a swirl of mist the crone's grey tresses
Curl round the cliff's edges. A sudden squall
And as if by magic a rainbow with its ghostly twin
Arc-light the gloom. I look up, but legs founder,
Bog-swallowed. I pluck my boots from sucking mud,
Dribble chill-peat from squeezed socks. A cold
Hag-land this, archaic, profound with paradox:
A sky high valley of origins and ends,
Dowager-queened; its wet dough unbaked even at
High solstice temperatures, when the sun's
Warm poultices cleanse for lowland harvesting.
A land of stagnancy, the feminine principle
Gone stale as unchanged the hag waits
Nursing ire between ice age and ice age.

VI
At the lake edge, on its necklace of brown erratics,
We attach the clicking reels to rods, tie flies
And whip them, wet or dry, onto the tarn's dark face.
Slowly, we edge westwards; but nothing takes 'till
By the mouth of an overflowing stream, small trout
Shoal. 'This is almost sinful,' Gabriel says
And we haul in the fighting half-pounders, brown
Backed, bellies peaty-bronze – the smallest we return.
A few, quick to detect masked hooks, reject
Our metal and spitting venomously out, smash
The surface.

VII
      Then, witch-magic, a surprise of fire.
A quick struggle of flame amid murky waters, like
Bright ecstatic echoes from the cauldron darkness.
'A char,' Gabriel shouts: an exotic, unsought
Arctic char, blue-backed, ruby speckled, its belly
Electric red – cold underworld survivor, a rare
Coin filched from the crone's black treasury;
A post-glacial relic awaiting with its hag-fosterer
The next ice-lurch – the white push southwards.

Potato

A shrunken pigmy's skull –
this tuber, soft as pulp,
found in the kitchen cupboard.

'Come and see this,' you called.

I bent, amazed at how its
wrinkled forehead had shot
two pale-violet antlers,
each over thirty inches long
stiffly up, vice-tight
between wall and shelf; and

further up to where a faint
star of light beaconed it
behind the kitchen sink.

Rootless, through the long night
of its dark abandonment,
as if, in secret life-protest,
some instinct deep within it

clicked like a protective
thermostat – at which, with
mystic intensity it stretched
all the stored energy of its
being – towards the star:

the one chink of hope in
an otherwise dark universe.

Summer Thunder

My sprint in from the garden
is beaten easily
by the first furious drops.

A shadow of anger darkens
my afternoon window
with dusky forebodings.

To read, I have to switch on
my kitchen lights
as, tensely, I listen to

a crackling barrage
that rattles on my roof-tiles;
then, the echoing roll

of an empty tar-barrel
up a stoney roadway.
Magnesium flashes go – snap

snap, snap as if our whole
community were under
aerial reconnaissance. Then

bombardment: a blitz
not of steel, thank God, but
a splattering of rain-grenades

which explode off concrete,
off car roofs, off house tops;
their bursting shrapnel

starting instant floods
in gateways, where gullies clog
and gutters cannot bear

their sudden overload.
Deep potholes fill and our summer road
becomes a stream-bed

down which – torrential waters.

As sudden as it came
the frown lifts
and light sprints back
from spent clouds.

Predator

When the limestone lake sank low this summer
again our paths crossed. You were prancing in water
chasing mallard when you glimpsed me down-wind
and stopped. Still as an old tree stump, I watched
across your marsh, where you seemed confused,
suspicious, could not trust your eyes; then off
you trotted along your shore in my full sight,
and again stopped and stared, still doubtful. Why
did I not move? And yet, you took no chances;
but before you left, as if to warn me off,
you lifted a red hind-leg to some green shrub.
And you were right, of course, not to trust me
though I only wished to view your habitat;
in your sharp nostrils I could stink at best;
and yet this place of rocks, ducks and lakes
would never be the same without you, anymore
than Eden would without its predator.

And then, at twelve o'clock on midsummer's night
there you were in the middle of the tar-road
right in the centre of my double-barrel lights
baffled, with no escape through six foot walls
which locked you from your forest, either side –
fully in my power now ... a pressure on the pedal;
but no, you trotted on ahead quite leisurely,
glancing sideways at my strange pursuing lights,
mystified; while I enjoyed that sense of power,
but more, the close-up spotlight on your trot
and colours. Dimming, or flashing, I let you feel
my will; and yet as another car approached,

I braked so you could find a gap through briars
back to your world. Wild fox, prowler of night,
long may you forage in these woods by the lake;
I would not have you otherwise – dead or tamed.
It's best your mystery remains, so live free,
but wary – between us there is secret enmity.

Obsessed with Lichens

And then there was that summer
he began a love affair
with lichens – almost an obsession
his eyes sought them everywhere:

on house roofs freckled
with their white ball-marks
or yellow or grey; and then there were
the summer snowballed walls

of Mayo and east Galway –
gate piers dripping their icy white,
parapets and gravestones
exquisitely enamelled orange, black.

How he pursued them
up steep Ben Awe and Scoltach;
stopping to photograph their
field survey maps, bright atlases.

And some stones, too,
which he'd collected for their
exotic patterns and colours,
he ferried home

in the boot of his car
to add their lichen petals
to his dull heather beds.
Now he calls these .....

his *stone flowers*.